Special Paint Techniques

The collage projects in this book combine traditional decoupage with painted accents and embellishments. Your creative collage project can be enhanced with a few simple painting techniques to create visually interesting multi-media creations.

The trick to mastering many painting skills is to choose the correct brushes. This guide will help you match the right brush to each technique used in the projects. Refer to it often!

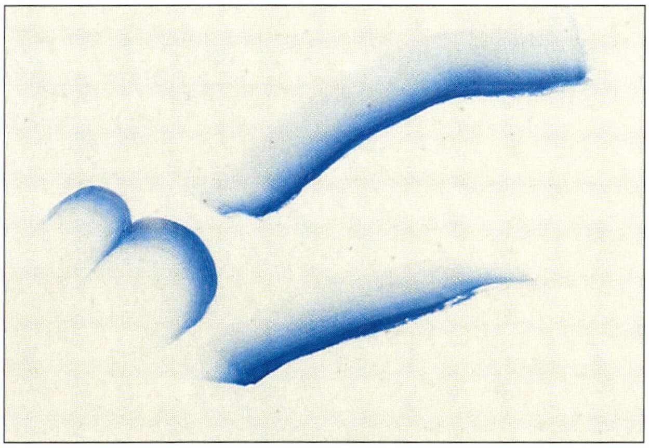

SHADING

Use a Royal Knight 7150 Shader 6 or 8, or 7190 Dagger $1/4$" or $3/8$".

Wet the brush, then blot lightly. Dip one side into your chosen color and blend well on a palette. Add J.W. etc. OpenTime Extender/Retarder to prevent paint from drying too quickly. Paint onto surface.

Aim for full color on the picture edge, gradually blending out to nothing, giving a soft shadow effect.

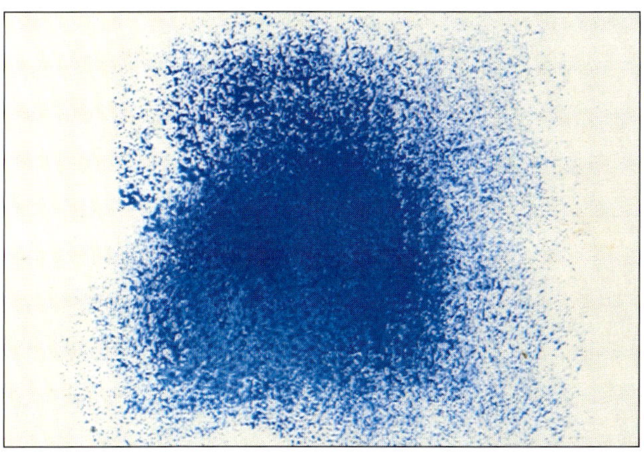

SPONGING

Wet a synthetic or natural sponge, then remove excess water. Work full-strength paint well into sponge, then dab color onto surface. TIP: More dabbing in one area will result in heavier paint application.

DRY BRUSHING

Use a Royal 5810 Flat Bristle 6 or 8 for smaller projects. Use a 10 or 12 for larger surfaces.

LINE WORK

Using a Royal Knight 7585 Script Liner #1, 2 or 4 and a thin mix of paint and water (the consistency of ink) and holding the brush upright with the tip just touching the surface, paint curls and swirls by moving the brush in both clockwise and counter-clockwise directions.

TIP: Use this method for outlining paper images.

VARNISHING

Many brushes may be used for this purpose. For example: Royal $3/4$" or 1" 1400 Series White Wash Goat Hair, or $3/4$" Aqualon Gold Taklon Varnish/Glaze Brush • Wet brush before varnishing, blot dry, then apply a liberal, even coat of varnish.

Basic Instructions

These steps explain the basic process of decoupage. Use these general instructions in conjunction with the projects on the following pages to create beautiful collaged pieces for your home and your family.

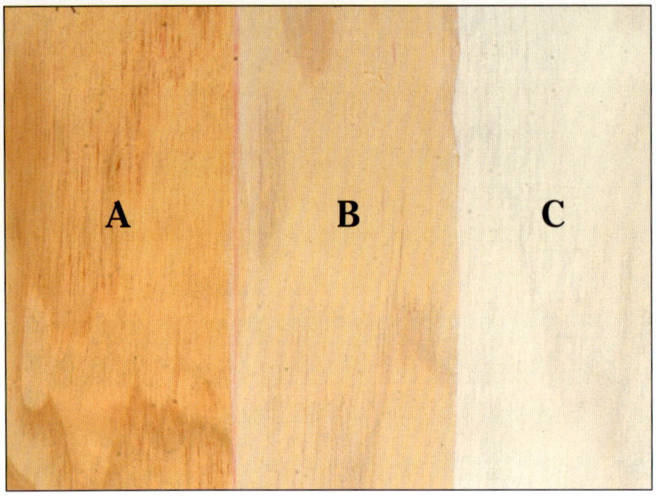

PREPARATION

Examine the raw wood piece. Nail holes or imperfections should be filled using J. W. etc. Wood Filler. Sand lightly with a medium grade sandpaper to smooth.

Wood surfaces should be sealed before painting. Several sealing products are available from J. W. etc., all of which do similar things. Choose products suitable to your planned project:

(A) First-Step is a clear wood sealer. I use this when I want to preserve the wood color or if I use a solid dark color.

(B) White Lightning is a clear sealer and white stain. It is ideal for all wood surfaces and gives a very smooth finish.

(C) UnderCover is a heavy gesso-type sealer and undercoat used mainly under white or light colored basecoat colors of paint.

Apply selected product to all wood surfaces using a bristle brush. Let dry, then sand lightly using medium grade sandpaper.

TIP: For a smoother surface, repeat this process.

BASECOAT PAINTING

Apply a light, even coat of paint. Let it dry. Sand the surface with a fine grade sandpaper. Repeat to achieve a solid, even layer of paint.

TIP: To avoid damage to the painted surface during subsequent steps, apply a thin layer of First-Step or clear sealer. Let sealer dry completely.

PREPARING PAPER

Using a soft glaze brush, apply a thin layer of J. W. etc. Decoupage Plus to both sides of the paper design. This strengthens the paper for cutting and gluing.

CUTTING

Carefully cut around the images using sharp scissors. Use small scissors with long straight shafts, or a sharp craft knife and cutting mat. The quality of the finished product relies on how well images are cut. Take your time to ensure a good result.

ARRANGING

Arrange the cut paper images on the painted project. Experiment a bit, first selecting the images you would most like to use, combining them with others and smaller pieces until you are happy with the design.

GLUING

J. W. etc. Decoupage Plus is made especially for this process. Brush liberally on back of the image. Place in position on the surface of the project. Remove excess glue, air bubbles and wrinkles in paper by massaging gently with fingers or brush. A brayer or hard rubber roller may also be used, working from center to edges of each image. Some images may overlap, so take care to glue the images in the correct order.

SEALING

When all images have been glued in place, brush over the entire surface with Decoupage Plus to provide a protective layer before finishing with varnish.

VARNISHING

Varnish is now applied to all surfaces. When dry, this provides a hard protective coating for your project. Choose a varnish suited to your project:

J. W. etc. Right-Step is a multi-purpose varnish, originally developed for decoupage. It dries to the touch in 15 minutes and also wet-sands well for a superb decorative finish.

Polyurethane Varnish is easy to apply. When dry, it is highly durable and hard.

Use a soft glaze brush to apply the varnish liberally to one surface at a time.

TIP: Dry and reapply several times to achieve a thick, protective coating. 3 or 4 coats will adequately seal and protect, but the more layers of varnish applied, the greater the quality of the final finish.

FINAL FINISH

Allow varnish time to harden before the final process. Dip wet and dry sandpaper into water and rub gently over the varnished surface to smooth.

Follow with a light but even rubbing of steel wool, to remove shiny patches in the varnish surface. Wipe the surface clean before applying a final coat of varnish.

TIP: If desired, apply a coat of J. W. etc. Finishing Wax.

KEY PLAQUE

SIZE: $5^{1}/_{4}$" x $7^{1}/_{4}$"

MATERIALS:

- *Artifacts* Paulo's Study Decoupage Paper
- *Walnut Hollow* Chippendale Pine Plaque
- *J. W. etc.* (UnderCover, Fruitwood Craftsman's Blend, Right-Step Matte Varnish, Decoupage Plus)
- *DecoArt* Americana Acrylic Paint (French Vanilla, Honey Brown, Warm White, Burnt Umber)
- Spattering tool or old toothbrush
- Brushes (bristle, foam, shader, varnish)

INSTRUCTIONS:

Prepare the wood plaque using UnderCover.

- Basecoat with French Vanilla, then dry brush with Honey Brown and Warm White.

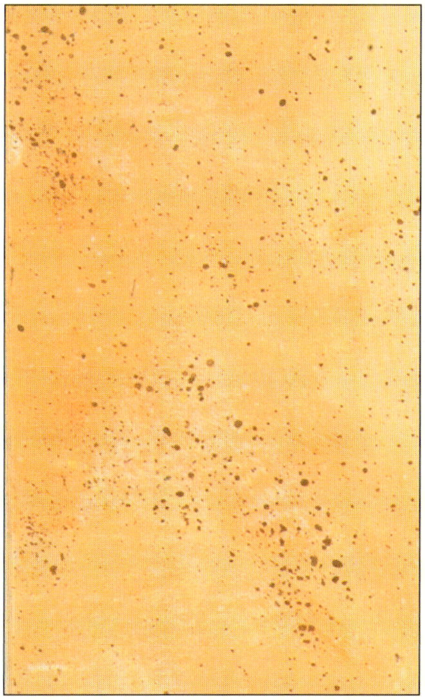

Using either a spatter tool or a toothbrush loaded with a watery mix of Burnt Umber and White, flick paint over the surface, giving an aged effect with fly specks.

Paint the edges of plaque Burgundy. • Following the general instructions, apply the key images as shown. • Using Burnt Umber, shade around one side and under all images to form shadows. • Antique the surface with Craftsman's Blend to complete the aging process. • To protect the plaque, use Right-Step Matte Varnish.

SIZE: 12 1/2" x 20 1/2"

MATERIALS:

Artifacts Vinrosa Decoupage Paper • *Walnut Hollow* Home Plate Oval Handle Serving Platter • *J.W. etc.* (UnderCover, Right-Step Satin Varnish, Decoupage Plus) • *DecoArt* Americana Acrylic Paint (Ultramarine Blue, Titanium White, Raw Sienna, Burnt Sienna, Burnt Umber) • Brushes (foam, bristle, #2 script liner, shader, varnish)

INSTRUCTIONS:

Prepare platter with UnderCover. Lightly draw a line dividing the platter in half. Paint the top section using an equal mix of Ultramarine Blue and Titanium White. Dry brush with White and a darker mix of Blue to make the cloudy pattern. Repeat for lower section using a Raw Sienna and White mix. Dry brush with Burnt Sienna. • Using a foam brush, paint platter edge Burnt Umber.

Following the general instructions, apply images from Vinrosa Decoupage Paper to platter.

Using a flat shader and a thin mix of Burnt Umber and water, paint under all images to form shadows. Using a #2 script liner, add fine outlines and curls around the grapes and olives. • Apply Right-Step Satin Varnish.

Vinrosa Serving Tray

Create a large luscious platter that is perfect for serving coffee, wine and cheese. It is as easy as paint, cut, glue and seal. Arrange grapes and olives to complement the beautiful design.

SIZE: 12" x 20"

MATERIALS:

Artifacts Lavender Blue Decoupage Paper • *Walnut Hollow* French Provincial Sign • *J.W. etc.* (First-Step Wood Sealer, Decoupage Plus, White Lightning, Matte Polyurethane Varnish) • *DecoArt* Americana Acrylic Paint (Colonial Blue, Summer Lilac, Silver Sage) • Brushes (3/8" dagger or shader, #4 script liner, foam, varnish) • Medium grade sandpaper

INSTRUCTIONS:

Prepare wood plaque with White Lightning. • In place of solid basecoat, apply second layer of White Lightning, thinning with water. This can be rubbed back with damp cloth or allowed to dry and sanded, revealing the color and grain of the wood.

Apply a coat of First-Step to seal the raw wood exposed with heavy sanding. • Follow the general instructions to apply images from Lavender Blue Decoupage Paper to the plaque. • Using a 3/8" dagger or shader and a watery mix of Summer Lilac, add accents to the flowers. Add Silver Sage accents to leaves.

Transfer lettering onto the plaque. Paint using a #4 script liner and Colonial Blue. When dry, sand using medium grade sandpaper to soften the lettering. • Apply a thin layer of Decoupage Plus and allow to dry. • Seal with matte varnish.

Welcome Plaque

Place this lovely plaque on the hall table next to the Guest book to welcome family and friends to your home. Choose motifs that match your decor, or carry a specific theme.

Decorative Cupboard

Use this cupboard in your home to store small items, or make one as a gift for your daughter or granddaughter. This cabinet is the perfect size for doll clothes.

SIZE:
$10^{1/4}$" x $10^{3/4}$" x 5" deep

MATERIALS:
Artifacts Lavender Blue Decoupage Paper • *Walnut Hollow* Doll Furniture Tuckaway Cubby • *J.W. etc.* (UnderCover, Right-Step Satin Varnish, Decoupage Plus) • *DecoArt* Americana Acrylic Paint (Cool White, Colonial Blue) • Brushes (foam, small script liner, varnish)

INSTRUCTIONS:
Prepare cupboard with UnderCover. Be certain the piece is well sanded and coated to achieve a solid White base. • Basecoat with Cool White. Reapply as necessary to achieve a solid cover of white.
Using a foam brush, edge the cupboard with Colonial Blue. Let dry, then sand heavily to reveal White paint.
Repeat on cupboard knobs.

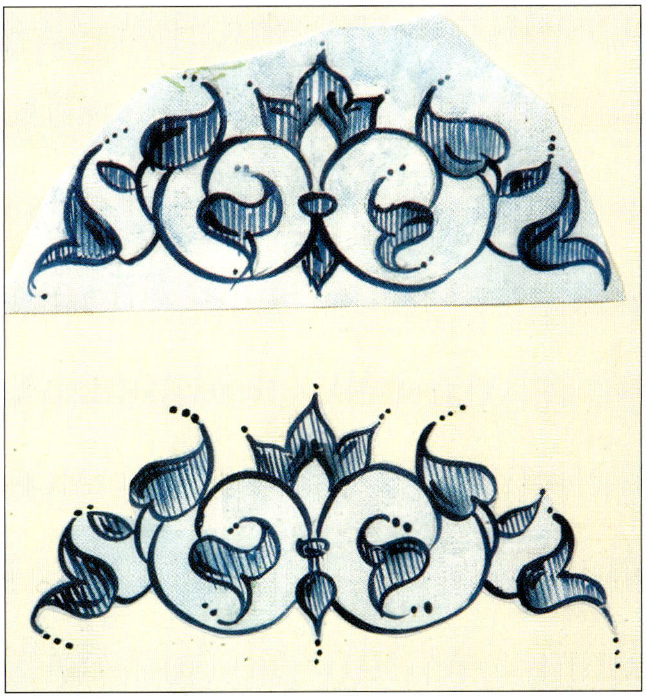

Following the general instructions, apply images from Lavender Blue Decoupage Paper to the cupboard. The paper design features small dots at the edges. Rather than cutting finely, remove them. After all images are glued and dry, the dots can be painted using a small brush and Colonial Blue. • Finish with Right-Step Satin.

Sailor's Delight Photo Frame

Ships Ahoy! You can almost hear the wind ruffling the sails in this delightful decoration for all the sailors in your family. Fill this frame with a fantasy sailboat and inspire dreams in a child's room.

SIZE: 7" x 9"

MATERIALS:

Artifacts Sailor's Delight Decoupage Paper • *Walnut Hollow* Frame with Oval Opening • *J.W. etc.* (UnderCover, Right-Step Satin Varnish, Decoupage Plus, First-Step Wood Sealer) • *DecoArt* Americana Acrylic Paints (Titanium White, Ultramarine Blue, Calico Red) • Masking tape • Brushes (foam, bristle, varnish)

INSTRUCTIONS:

Prepare the frame with UnderCover. Paint both sides of the frame with White. Apply as many coats as necessary to achieve complete coverage.

Using tape, mask out evenly spaced stripes on the front and back of frame. Be certain all tape edges are well secured to avoid paint bleed. Using a mix of Blue and White, paint between the tape, covering all White areas. (Adding too much water to paint could cause it to bleed under the tape.)

Let dry. Remove tape carefully to reveal solid Blue and White stripes. Dry brush over the entire surface with White to give a soft, weathered look. • Paint the outer edge of frame using a foam brush and Calico Red. Follow the general instructions to apply images from Sailor's Delight Decoupage Paper to the frame. Finish frame with Right-Step Satin varnish.

Tropical Trinket Box

Flowers are a favorite gift to give and receive, especially on Mother's Day. Make this box for Mom and give her flowers that won't fade away.

SIZE: 6 1/4" x 6 1/4" x 6" high

MATERIALS:

Artifacts Tropicana Decoupage Paper • *Walnut Hollow* Ball Foot Personal Box • *J.W. etc.* (UnderCover, Polyurethane Gloss Varnish, Decoupage Plus, Violet Pearl Artistic Finish) • *DecoArt* Americana Acrylic Paint (Ultramarine Blue, Titanium White, Lavender) • Brushes (#2 script liner, foam, bristle, varnish)

INSTRUCTIONS:

Prepare the box using UnderCover. Basecoat using equal parts of Ultramarine Blue and White.

Paint the ball feet with Lavender.

1. Using the same brush and a swirling motion, dry brush White randomly over all surfaces.

2. With a liner brush and a thin mix of Blue, cover each surface with swirls and spirals.

3. Follow the general instructions to apply images from Tropicana Decoupage Paper to the box.

4. Using a #2 script liner brush and a thin mix of White, add outlines and accents to flowers and leaves. • Coat the ball feet and knob using Violet Pearl Artistic Finish. Apply a second and a third coat as necessary. Brush a bit on each side of box for a pearly finish. • Finish using Polyurethane Gloss Varnish.

Flower Power Memory Album

Peace! The 60's are back! Recapture the spirit of the "flower power" age with bright neon colors and motifs while providing a home for all those photos from the "sit-in".

BACK COVER

SIZE: 10" x 12"

MATERIALS:

Artifacts Flower Power Decoupage Paper • *Walnut Hollow* Contemporary Memory Album Cover • *J.W. etc.* (UnderCover, Polyurethane Gloss Varnish, First-Step Wood Sealer, Decoupage Plus) • *DecoArt* Americana Acrylic Paint (Vivid Violet, Jack-O-Lantern Orange, Lamp Black) • *Plaid* Royal Coat Gold Foil Kit • Brushes (foam, varnish)

INSTRUCTIONS:

Prepare all surfaces with UnderCover. Paint two surfaces Vivid Violet, and two surfaces Orange. Dry brush Orange over Violet and Violet over Orange. • Using a foam brush, paint the edges of album Lamp Black. • Follow the general instructions to apply images from Flower Power Decoupage Paper to the album.

INSIDE FRONT COVER

INSIDE BACK COVER

The front of the album is made of two pieces, and the heart image overlaps the join. With the image in position, mark it by rubbing along the edge to form a crease. Use the crease as cutting line. Glue the heart in place, making sure the album pieces are correctly aligned. • Finish the album with glossy varnish.

Add gold accents to the front cover using a foil kit, and following the manufacturer's instructions.

Room Door Plaque

Show off the unique style of each child in your home with individual plaques made just for them. Use motifs that express their personality, and of course, choose their favorite colors.

SIZE: 5 1/4" x 7 1/4"

MATERIALS:

Artifacts Flower Power Decoupage Paper • *Walnut Hollow* Basswood French Corner Plaque • *J.W. etc.* (UnderCover, Polyurethane Gloss Varnish, Decoupage Plus) • *DecoArt* Americana Acrylic Paint (Lamp Black, Bright Green)• *Plaid* Royal Coat Gold Foil Kit • Brushes (foam, #4 liner, varnish) • Chalk or pencil

INSTRUCTIONS:

Prepare the surface with UnderCover. Basecoat with Bright Green. Paint the edges with Lamp Black. • Following the general instructions, apply images from Flower Power Decoupage Paper to the plaque. • When dry, draw a name lightly with chalk or with a pencil. Paint name with a #4 liner brush and Lamp Black. • Apply Polyurethane Gloss Varnish. • Add gold accents with a foil kit, following the manufacturer's directions.

Tropicana Frame

Imagine yourself in the tropics. These sunny flowers will make you smile every time you see them.

SIZE: 11" x 12 1/2"

MATERIALS:

Artifacts Tropicana Decoupage Paper • *Walnut Hollow* Rectangle Frame • *J.W. etc.* (UnderCover, Right-Step Gloss Varnish, Decoupage Plus) • *DecoArt* Americana Acrylic Paint (Festive Green, Cadmium Yellow, Titanium White, Bright Orange) • Brushes (foam, #2 script liner, bristle, varnish)

INSTRUCTIONS:

Prepare a wood frame using UnderCover. Basecoat the frame with Festive Green and Cadmium Yellow, adding a touch of White to soften the color. Dry brush Yellow from the center of frame, gradually blending into Green. Using a foam brush, paint the inside and outside edges of frame Bright Orange. • Following the general instructions, apply images from Tropicana Decoupage Paper to the frame. Before sealing, add outlines and accents to the flowers and leaves using a #2 script liner brush and a thin mix of White and water. • Finish with Right-Step Gloss Varnish.

Faux Mosaic Clock

Bring the warmth of Mexico into your home with this Southwest style mosaic. The happy colors and fun patterns brighten any time of day.

SIZE: 12" x 20"

MATERIALS:

Artifacts Mosaic Star Decoupage Paper • *Walnut Hollow (*Pine Tavern Sign, 3 Piece Clock Kit) • *J.W. etc.* (First-Step Wood Sealer, Right-Step Matte Varnish, Decoupage Plus) • *DecoArt* Americana Acrylic Paints (French Grey Blue, Lamp Black, Titanium White) • *Plaid* Royal Coat Clear Dimensional Magic • Brushes (foam, bristle, shader, varnish)

INSTRUCTIONS:

Prepare wood with First-Step Wood Sealer. • Using French Grey Blue, paint the central section. Dry brush with Black and White to blend the painted background with the paper color. Thin paint slightly with water and cover the top and bottom sections. When dry, sand heavily to reveal some raw wood underneath.

Following the general instructions, apply images from Mosaic Star Decoupage Paper to the clock. • When dry, shade around each tile image with Black. • Apply 3 - 4 coats of Right-Step Matte Varnish.

Let dry. • Apply Dimensional Magic carefully to each painted tile, giving the effect of real ceramic mosaic tiles. Let dry. • Add the clock movement, hands and numerals.

Faux Mosaic Drink Coasters

Make a clever gift. Coasters are always a useful item to protect any table or wood surface.

SIZE: 3 3/4" x 3 3/4"

MATERIALS:

Walnut Hollow Small Square Pine Plaques as surface.

INSTRUCTIONS:

Prepare coasters in the same method as the Faux Mosaic Clock above.

TIP: To finish, use Polyurethane Matte Varnish instead of Dimensional Magic.

Patchwork Tray

Plaid papers are so much fun to work with, and so easy too! Use them to make the patchwork collage on this tray. Choose colors that coordinate with your central motif, and enjoy this lighthearted project. It will brighten up any kitchen or dining room.

SIZE: 11 1/2" x 15 1/2"

MATERIALS:

Artifacts Decorative Foliage Decoupage Paper • *Walnut Hollow* Chippendale Tray • *J.W. etc.* (White Lightning or First-Step Wood Sealer, Crackle Medium, OpenTime, Fruitwood Craftsman Blend Stain, Polyurethane Matte Varnish) • *DecoArt* Americana Acrylic Paint (Olde Gold, Warm White, Forest Glade Green, Burnt Umber) • Brushes (bristle, flat, foam, #4 script liner, varnish)

INSTRUCTIONS:

Prepare the tray using First-Step Wood Sealer.

Paint the inside of tray with Olde Gold. When dry, apply a medium coat of Crackle Medium with a bristle brush, using short criss-cross strokes. Leave the rim of the tray free of Crackle Medium. Let dry.

Thin Warm White with OpenTime and a little water. Apply with a bristle brush.

TIPS: Overworking the paint will spoil the result. As the top coat dries, cracks will appear.

Following the general instructions, apply images from Decorative Foliage Decoupage Paper to the tray.

Cover the rim of the tray with randomly cut pieces of patterned paper to give a patchwork look.

Using a #4 script liner and Forest Glade Green, cover the joins between the paper patches. Shade around the edges with a flat brush.

Using a foam brush and Forest Glade Green, paint the edge of tray.

Using Burnt Umber, add lines and accents to the wreath.

Seal completely with First-Step. When dry, apply Craftsman's Blend with a damp cloth, rubbing gently in a rotating motion, giving an aged or antiqued look.

Finish with Polyurethane Matte Varnish.

Writing Box

Express your vision of Victorian elegance when you choose the motifs to cover your stationery box. This project makes a useful desk ornament for your den or office. Or, make it in motifs to match the room decor, and place it in your guest room.

SIZE: 10 1/4" x 10 1/4" x 5" high

MATERIALS:
Artifacts Paulo's Study Decoupage Paper • *Walnut Hollow* Square Lancaster Box • *J.W. etc.* (UnderCover, Right-Step Satin Varnish, Fruitwood Craftsman's Blend, Decoupage Plus, Crackle Medium, Finishing Wax, Antique Gold and Aztec Gold Artistic Finish) • *DecoArt* Americana Acrylic Paints (French Vanilla, Honey Brown, Warm White, Burnt Umber, Traditional Raw Sienna) • Brushes (foam, dagger or shader, bristle, varnish) • White craft glue • Tissue paper • Sandpaper

TOP OF BOX INSTRUCTIONS:
Prepare the lid using UnderCover. Paint with French Vanilla. Let dry. Dry brush in a criss-cross motion with Honey Brown and Warm White. • Using a foam brush, paint the edge of lid with Burnt Umber. • Following the general instructions, apply images from Paulo's Study Decoupage Paper to the lid. • When dry, add accents to images with a thin mix of Burnt Umber and water using a dagger or shader brush. • Apply crackle to the entire surface using a bristle brush. Let dry.

Apply a medium coat of Right-Step Varnish using a glaze brush. Let dry. As the varnish dries, cracks will appear. • Apply Craftsman's Blend using a damp cloth and a circular motion to reveal the crackled surface and give an aged look. Wipe away excess to achieve the desired color. • Cover the piece with satin varnish. Let dry for 24 hours. Rub with finishing wax to give a soft luster.

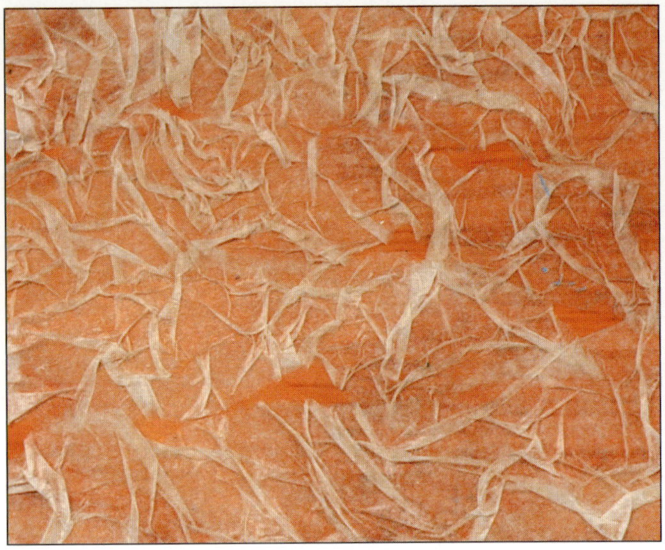

BASE OF BOX INSTRUCTIONS: Do not seal the wood Mix equal parts craft glue and water. Tear strips of tissue paper and crumple. Brush the outer surface of box with the glue mix. Uncrumple tissue and place it on the glued surface. Remove air bubbles, but leave wrinkles. Continue until all sides are covered.

TIP: The glue will dry to a clear, hard surface. Any rough edges may be lightly sandpapered.

Paint the box inside and out with Traditional Raw Sienna. Dry brush with a mixture of Warm White and Burnt Umber. • Using a foam brush, paint the ball feet and edges of box with Burnt Umber. • Using a bristle brush, apply Antique Gold Artistic Finish, brushing in a criss-cross motion. Repeat using Aztec Gold. Apply to ball feet and edges. • When dry, varnish with Right-Step Varnish.

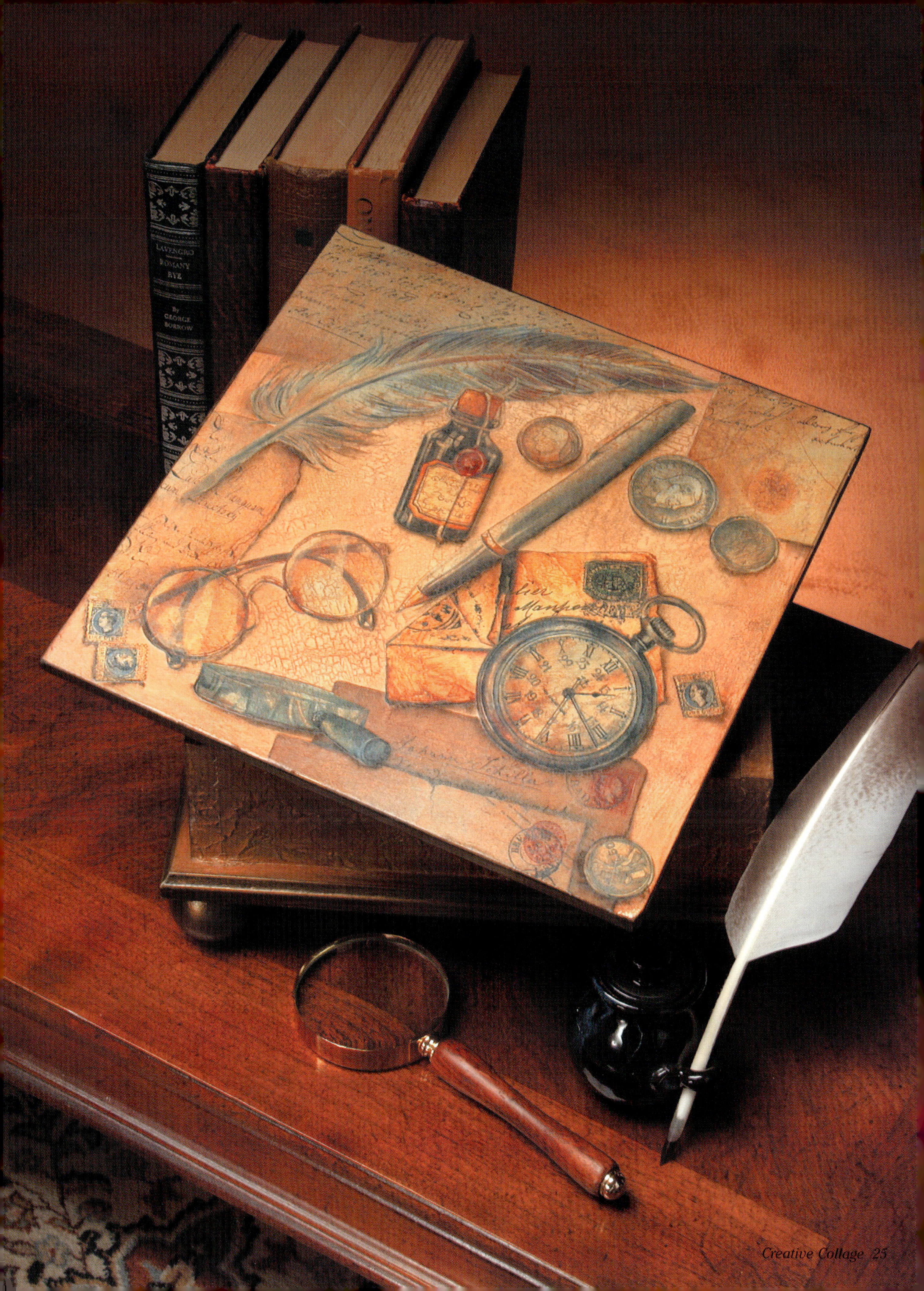

Oriental Clock

Oriental motifs add a rich, regal feeling to a room. Decorate this clock with your favorite Eastern symbols.

SIZE: 11" diameter

MATERIALS:
Artifacts Geisha and the Crane Decoupage Paper • *Walnut Hollow (*Round Clock Plaque, Clock Movement Kit) • *J.W. etc.* (First-Step Wood Sealer, Polyurethane Gloss Varnish, Decoupage Plus, OpenTime) • *DecoArt* Americana Acrylic Paint (Lamp Black, Spun Gold) • Plastic wrap • Brushes (foam, varnish)

INSTRUCTIONS:
Prepare wood using First-Step Wood Sealer. Basecoat with Lamp Black.

Mix 2 parts of Spun Gold with 1 part each OpenTime and water. Paint a light coat to completely cover the surface. While still wet, cover the surface with plastic wrap and move it around, making wrinkles on the surface. Remove immediately to reveal a textured finish. Let dry.

Following the general instructions, apply images from Geisha and the Crane Decoupage Paper to the clock. • Finish using Polyurethane Gloss Varnish. • Add clock movement, hands and numerals.

Classic Beauties Wall Plaque

Here's a great way to display those exquisite images or old photographs. Make several and create your own collection to display in your home.

SIZE: 11 1/2" x 14 1/2"

MATERIALS:

Artifacts Classic Beauties Decoupage Paper • *Walnut Hollow* Basswood Oval Plaque • *J.W. etc.* (UnderCover, Polyurethane Gloss Varnish, Antique Gold and Sparkling Copper Artistic Finish, Decoupage Plus) • *DecoArt* Flesh Americana Acrylic Paint • Brushes (foam, varnish)• Synthetic Sponge • Steel wool • Sandpaper

INSTRUCTIONS:

Prepare the plaque using UnderCover. Basecoat the frame moulding with Flesh. Let dry. • Using a sponge, apply Sparkling Copper and let dry. Apply a second coat for deeper color. • Using the plaque as a template, center it on image, to mark the cutting line.

Following the general instructions, apply image from Classic Beauties Decoupage Paper to the center of the plaque. • When dry, the edges may be trimmed if required. With a small piece of sandpaper, carefully rub the edges to smooth and remove excess paper. • Using a synthetic sponge and Antique Gold, color the outer area of the image. Apply a second coat, sponging over the outer frame, highlighting the contours. • Apply polyurethane gloss varnish. When dry, remove gloss from the frame by rubbing with fine steel wool, leaving the image area shiny.

Geisha Brooch

Wear this brooch with pride when friends ask "Where did you buy that? ...When did you get back from Japan?"

SIZE: 3" diameter

MATERIALS:

Artifacts Geisha and the Crane Decoupage Paper • *J.W. etc.* (First-Step Sealer, Polyurethane Gloss Varnish, Decoupage Plus, OpenTime) • *DecoArt* Americana Acrylic Paint (Lamp Black, Spun Gold) • Large wood button • Pin back • Adhesive • Brushes (foam, varnish)

INSTRUCTIONS:

Prepare with First-Step. Paint Lamp Black • Mix 2 parts of Spun Gold with 1 part each OpenTime and water. Apply to the edges of wood button with a foam brush. • Following the general instructions, apply image from Geisha and the Crane Decoupage Paper to the button. To glue image over the curved surface, clip from the outer edge toward the center, avoiding face.

Finish with several coats of polyurethane gloss.

Attach a pin back.

Country Blooms Drop Side Table

Make the perfect side table to hold your tea after a morning of gardening. Set your favorite chair next to this quaint table so you can look out the window and admire your handiwork.

SIZE: 18 3/4" x 18 3/4" x 23 1/4" high

MATERIALS:

Artifacts Country Blooms Decoupage Paper • *Walnut Hollow* Drop Leaf Table • *J.W. etc.* (UnderCover, Polyurethane Satin Varnish, Decoupage Plus, First-Step Wood Sealer) • *DecoArt* Americana Acrylic Paint (Warm White, Country Blue, Moon Yellow, Vivid Violet) • Pencil • Eraser • Sandpaper • Ruler • Brushes (foam, shader, varnish)

INSTRUCTIONS:

Prepare all surfaces with UnderCover. • Basecoat the table top with Warm White, using as many coats as necessary to achieve even coverage.

Using a pencil and ruler, lightly mark diagonal lines across the table top. • Using a watery mix of Moon Yellow, shade along each line. Turn the table around and shade on the other side of lines.

When dry, erase any pencil lines. • Measure the lines crossing others at right angles, forming a lattice pattern. Repeat process of shading, completing a lattice pattern. Erase all pencil lines. • Using a foam brush, paint the edge of table, legs and lower shelf Country Blue, following the grain. Let dry. Sand heavily with the grain, revealing the White undercoat.

Following the general instructions, apply images from Country Blooms Decoupage Paper to the table. When images are glued and dry, shade under each pot with a watery mix of Vivid Violet. • Finish the table with Polyurethane Satin Varnish.

Classic Beauties Lamp Table

Grape leaves entwine your favorite image of classic beauty, making a wonderful addition to any room. Set a doily and lamp on this table, or use it to display your favorite collection.

SIZE: $16^{3}/_{4}$" x $16^{3}/_{4}$" x $27^{1}/_{2}$" high

MATERIALS:

Artifacts Classic Beauties Decoupage Paper • *Walnut Hollow* Lamp Table • *J.W. etc.* (White Lightning, Right-Step Satin Varnish, Copper Colored Wax, Antique Green Artistic Finish) • *DecoArt* Americana Acrylic Paint (Colonial Blue, Ocean Green, Burnt Umber, Warm White) • Synthetic sponge • Brushes (foam, #4 script liner, varnish)

INSTRUCTIONS:

Prepare the table with White Lightning. • Basecoat tabletop and legs with Colonial Blue, adding touches of Ocean Green and blending.

Following the general instructions, apply images from Classic Beauties Decoupage Paper on the table. Glue only the large central image. • In each corner of a palette, place dabs of Colonial Blue, Ocean Green, Warm White and Burnt Umber. Using a sponge and a stipple brush, blend the colors, working from the picture edge, blending gradually out into the background.

Sponge Antique Green Artistic Finish randomly over the tabletop, concentrating more where ivy leaves will be placed. Glue leaves in place.

Using a #4 script liner and Burnt Umber, add accents and curls. Seal and let dry.

Apply Copper wax by lightly rubbing along the edges of the tabletop and the legs. • Finish table with Right-Step Satin Varnish.

LA CÔTE D'AZUR
CANNES
HOTEL ROYAL
ISTHME
DE DARIEN
GOLFO DE PANAMA
Isles Royales
DU SUD
HOTEL D'EUROPE
LAUSANNE
CAIRO
Palace Hôtel
Copenhague
HOTEL CRISTINA
SEVILLA
DAPEST
SÜDBAHNHOTEL
SEMMERING
FRANCE